CONTEMPORAR
IN T

C000075923

EDITED BY GIOV

The series "Contemporary Architecture in Turin"
has been realised thanks to support from
the Urban Center Metropolitano of Turin.

www.urbancenter.to.it

LUCA DAL POZZOLO
MICHELA BENENTE

BAROQUE
300 years old and as young as ever

UMBERTO ALLEMANDI & C.
TURIN ~ LONDON ~ VENICE ~ NEW YORK

We should like to thank Vera Comoli, Giuseppe Dardanello,
Marco Demarie, Giovanni Ferrero, Mirella Macera,
Alberto Vanelli and Sergio Scamuzzi for having agreed to be interviewed
and for the invaluable ideas and information they have provided.
Vera Comoli, who worked on these issues in fundamental volumes,
gave us the first drafts, with her corrections and annotations,
shortly before she left us forever. It is to her that we humbly dedicate this little book.

Thanks also to the Soprintendenza per i Beni Architettonici e il Paesaggio
del Piemonte for their help and the materials provided.

English translation
Simon Turner

On the cover
Jenny Holzer, *Xenon for Torino*, 2003.
Light installation on the facade of Palazzo Carignano. Photo by Paolo Pellion.

Contents

The destiny of the Baroque
LUCA DAL POZZOLO

THE BAROQUE AND THE MULTIPLE CITY

Turin is certainly a Baroque city although, like all metropolitan cities, it has a complex and multifaceted identity: a Roman city, an industrial city, long referred to as a "one-company town", a technological city and a cultural city by strategic vocation for the past twenty years, an Olympic and - now - a post-Olympic city.

The gradual transformation that has taken place over the centuries has led to inevitable losses, but it has also strengthened the city's identity. This is not just because layer has been added to layer, but also because every transformation, every addition, does not eliminate the past but simply changes the present and future directions, just as it transforms and relativises the events of the past and the sense of historic heritage we find before us. In the words of Bernardo Secchi:

> Separating the flow of history into periods, saying when each one started and when each one ends - and why - and telling the story of its most important aspects, is a way of thinking about time and reconstructing it while looking for the meaning of its passing. This operation is never innocent, all the more so when the time we reconstruct is so close to us that it is still filled with our own passions.[1]

In a sense, the argument sustained in these pages is that the Baroque is still very close to us and capable of mobilising our passions - to use the words that Secchi applied to the twentieth century - challenging our ability and intelligence to make best use of a legacy that is still alive and dynamic.

It is thus less ingenuous than it might seem to ask oneself what sense it makes today to reflect on the Baroque identity of Turin and what this might mean for the future vocation of the city. One answer is immediately clear: a city that has made its culture and cultural heritage strategic elements in its approach to future development cannot afford to neglect one of the fundamental periods of its history and urban identity. This is not just because - to paraphrase Borges - we all create our own predecessors, but also because the heritage we have been bequeathed by the Baroque in terms of architecture and city layout is still a core feature that is very much present in the city's material and immaterial make-up. We have been left an entire city by the Baroque, a "young city" as Vera Comoli Mandracci maintained, just three centuries old, and yet complete and still recognisable today. The construction of the capital city of the Duchy of Savoy and then of the Kingdom as from the age of Filiberto was tenaciously continued throughout the seventeenth and eighteenth centuries. It was guided by the structural vision of an absolutist State that subjected the entire territory to its designs. Its military power and the magnificence of its architecture were to convey the grandeur of the master project, and the works being undertaken were to be made known in order to create an image of the future city as though it had already been made.

As a result, within the space of just two centuries a material heritage (the urban and territorial structure, and the monuments and architectural fabric) and an immaterial heritage (the vision of the capital and its region, and the elements of its identity) were both created. Still today, this poses the city questions, issues, challenges and resources of extreme importance for its future development, as well as a whole range of problems that end up on the agenda of public and private decision makers, and indeed of the entire population.

It is from this angle that we shall examine the attention, inattention and attitudes towards the urban and architectural heritage of the Baroque. We shall follow the irregular fault lines, which are sometimes apparent, sometimes unseen, in the decisions and considerations concerning the future of the city, from the post-war period to the present day. It should be pointed out that the commitment and interest of Italian and foreign historians is anything but irregular when it comes to architecture and art, for since the war a vast and detailed wealth of information has been acquired: this now constitutes a key resource in the process of promoting the heritage of the Baroque. These well-established and extensive historical studies and surveys are one of the aspects that makes the Baroque age so close to us and, in the issues that this great architectural heritage raises, truly contemporary.

THE CITY AND ITS VISION

The Baroque city and its territory are still profoundly influenced by the plan for absolutist power[2] which gave not only the city but also a region that was densely populated (at least for that time) an extensive network of built-up areas. It almost suggested an extensive conglomeration, as we can see in the words of Giovanni Botero, who wrote in the early years of the seventeenth century:

> It has become a town so populous that the response given by a Piedmontese knight was by no means impertinent when he was asked by a Venetian gentleman what "Piamonte" was, saying that it is a city three hundred miles round.[3]

Under Emanuele Filiberto in the second half of the sixteenth century, Turin underwent a process of transformation that made it a capital city, first with the construction of the Cittadella, designed by Francesco Paciotto da Urbino, and later with repeated extensions along the new axes and around the new "command zone" which had its centre in what is now Piazza Castello. A succession of town-planning schemes by Ascanio Vitozzi, Ercole Negro di Sanfront, and Carlo and Amedeo di Castellamonte expanded on each other under Carlo Emanuele I, Vittorio Amedeo I, Carlo Emanuele II and Vittorio Amedeo II, and also included the work of Filippo Juvarra.

Along the main lines of communication outside the city walls, the territory was in the meanwhile being shaped around the royal residences and hunting lodges. These were authentic strongholds of authority and power at the local level, as well as a "*Corona di Delizie*", or "Crown of Delights", as Castellamonte put it, which consisted of hubs in the network planned and designed for governing the territory (fig. 1).

> The organisation of the system into rigid, intersecting territorial areas was based on a radiating relationship between the capital and the external residences. This formed part of a conceptual process that related the capital city to the prince's lands.[4]

This ambitious scheme for the capital city and for domination of the territory was illustrated and conveyed to the leading courts of Europe by

1. "Hunting Map", 1761-1762. Map illustrating absolutist planning in the city and its territory (detail). Turin, Archivio di Stato.

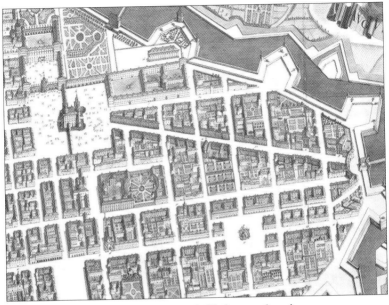

2. Gio Battista Borgonio, plan of the city, detail of the 'command zone' in *Theatrum Sabaudiae*, 1682.

the *Theatrum Sabaudiae*, which was published in Amsterdam in 1682. This plan focused "on the squares, buildings, churches, and residences of the capital, but also on the towns of the Duchy, which were to create a historical and political portrait to reveal its true identity in its modern entirety, and not just in celebratory terms."[5]

Through its engravings, the *Theatrum* portrayed a capital city (fig. 2) built to a strict design and with a powerful sense of unity in its building fronts. Almost a palace-city governed by a design that unified the urban scale and that of its architecture, without intentionally distinguishing between works that were already complete and those that were only planned, between the state of the art and the vision, for both the urban environment and the Crown of Delights. In actual fact Guarino Guarini, with his buildings and churches, and then Filippo Juvarra both worked in the opposite direction, moving away from this idea of uniformity that borders on monotony. They did so by giving places of power a hierarchical position, varying the architecture within a standard framework, and end-

3. Bernardo Bellotto, "View of Turin from the Bastion Verde", 1745 (detail). Turin, Galleria Sabauda.

ing up by pursuing the dream of the modern "capitol" inspired by Vittorio Amedeo II.[6] The incompleteness and the failure of this vision were made quite clear by Bellotto in his view of Turin now in the Galleria Sabauda:

> Bernardo Bellotto [fig. 3] has given us a demystifying snapshot of the contradictions to be found in the building site of modern Turin. The immediacy of the reality he portrays avoids any celebratory flattery in his unusual choice of a view from the Dora area beyond the walls, in the sharp midmorning light of late spring.[7]

The back of the royal palace (Palazzo Reale), the dome of Guarini's chapel of the Holy Shroud, and Juvarra's crowning on the bell tower reveal the fragmentary nature of a design that would never be recomposed. The Crown of Delights was never realised in a unified manner either,

4. Giovanni Paolo Pannini, "View of Rivoli Castle from the South", 1724.
Castle of Racconigi.

but instead in a number of takes. (This 'Crown' comprised the castles of
Rivoli, Mirafiori, Valentino, Moncalieri, the *vigna* of Madama Reale,
Viboccone at Regio Parco and Venaria [according to Castellamonte's
indications in 1672], to which the residences of Agliè, Racconigi and
Pollenzo were added.) Building yards were abandoned and construction
work started on new residences. As complex historical affairs unfolded,
the courts were transferred, leaving many of the buildings unfinished.
Venaria, the "*Porta delle Delizie*" (Gate of Delights) and the last, in
chronological order, in Castellamonte's 'Crown' was modified by a
number of different designs that changed its orientation and layout: in the
end, this led to a gigantic area that remained unfinished and disturbing-
ly asymmetrical. Juvarra's new design for the great visual axis that unites
Superga and Rivoli along what is now Corso Francia never saw the completion of the castle in Rivoli. This was to be a royal palace outside the

capital city and more than just a 'residence of delights'. Here the titanic enterprise of remodelling the heights to form an enormous garden with terraces leading down (fig. 4) was never made, although the Stupinigi hunting lodge (Palazzina di Caccia) was fully completed.

Partly as a result of the difference between what was planned and what was built – between what was engraved in the late seventeenth century and what actually appeared later – it is hard not to see the *Theatrum* through modern eyes as a marketing ploy on a grand scale. It seems as though it was made to give credit to the power of the State of Savoy through its town-planning projects and its architecture. And yet, at the same time, we can see a very different revelation in Bellotto's painting, which shows the actual state of the art behind the rhetoric of this vision. Even so, if we continue the modern parallel, the *Theatrum* was not just a marketing operation and a form of celebration; it reveals a broad vision of power and a way of governing a region. Though this vision was never completed, it was continued and built in many parts, extending its influence on the layout of the city at least until the early nineteenth century.

The *Theatrum* shows a global vision of the city and the surrounding territory, and a remodelling of the urban layout involving past, present and future, reducing everything to carefully planned order. Yet this was the very moment in which some of the masterpieces of Baroque architecture and, in particular, the works of Juvarra were going against the tide. They arose out of a confrontation with the limitations of the existing fabric, and out of the need to bear in mind what had already been built, while introducing innovation not to destroy but to reuse what was already there.[8] Within this authoritarian scheme, and within the mechanisms of absolutist planning, we find complexities and contradictions that do not however prevent this overall plan from being gradually brought to life and influencing the directions that urban development would later take.

From the early nineteenth century, the new schemes had to examine how to link up to this plan, how to continue its layout and road directions. They intended to create a new overall vision of the city, no longer confined within the city walls, but extending out towards a powerful and compact urbanisation of the territory.

The destiny of the Baroque

Baroque studies and research have enjoyed uninterrupted favour ever since the last war. At least six large exhibitions have helped focus on the enormous artistic legacy: in 1963 there was the *Barocco piemontese* exhibition curated by Vittorio Viale; in 1966 *Filippo Juvarra architetto e scenografo* also curated by Vittorio Viale; in 1967 *Bernardo Vittone architetto*, organised by Nino Carboneri and Vittorio Viale; in 1989 *Diana Trionfatrice* curated by Michela di Macco and Giovanni Romano; in 1995 *Juvarra. Architetto delle capitali da Torino a Madrid 1714-1736* curated by Vera Comoli Mandracci and Andreina Griseri with Beatriz Blanco Esquivias; and in 1999 *The Triumph of the Baroque* curated by Henry Millon.

There have been continuous studies since the 1950s, with work by Wittkower and his students in Turin and Piedmont; publications by Passanti, Portoghesi and Carboneri on Guarini, Vittone and Vitozzi; the fundamental *Metamorfosi del Barocco* by Andreina Griseri and the volume by Richard Pommer; studies by Cavallari-Murat and in-depth analyses of the history of town-planning in Turin by Vera Comoli Mandracci; studies by Roberto Gabetti and by Carlo Olmo; essays by Vera Comoli Mandracci and Costanza Roggero Bardelli in *Storia di Torino*, a catalogue of Juvarra's works by Gianfranco Gritella; essays by Dardanello on the architecture of Turin and his translation of Pommer's book. This is but a hasty list of some of the studies that have accumulated over the years, but it gives an idea of the quantity of research and knowledge compiled in the space of just over fifty years.

Despite the boom in studies, however, there still remain prejudices and mistrust of the Baroque at not marginal levels of public opinion, as well as in the way in which, in some cases, art history is taught in schools today. A counter-reformist involution, it is viewed as an "infesting" architecture when it remodels previous buildings, forming a less legitimate layer than that of the Renaissance - though it must be said that no complaints are heard when this overlaps the Middle Ages - while the Baroque entangles in superfluous, supposedly "tropical" additions. These are all prejudices that seem to echo the amazement of the past, when there was much debate among travellers at the time of Guarini and Juvarra. They expressed either admiration or condemnation when faced with the daring architectural experiments that were being carried out in Piedmont and in Turin. This is how engraver Charles Nicolas Cochin expressed himself in 1758:

> The architectural taste that reigns in this city must in no way serve as an example. Nevertheless, a cold and sterile mind might yet benefit from it and make good use of some clever trick by subjecting it to a wiser taste in order to provide a useful asset when ancient architecture might appear too severe.[9]

There was however some recognition of and admiration for the linguistic experiments that were finding fertile terrain for their development in a 'new' city. One crucial opportunity for post-war rediscovery by the broader public of the architectural and artistic heritage of the Baroque came with the "Italia '61" celebrations for the centenary of the Unification of Italy. At the end of the event, Marziano Bernardi wrote:

> Some thought it would not be proper to recall the institution of the Subalpine Parliament and the democratic determination of the first Italian parliament at a time when the facade of Palazzo Madama [fig. 5], where the "cry of pain" had first resounded, was falling to pieces. This led to the fa-

5. Turin, Palazzo Madama. Juvarra's facade after recent restoration.

mous allocation by the government of 1.12 billion lire for the restoration of the "historic castles of Piedmont" and, towards the end of 1959, came the request that the Soprintendenza ai Monumenti in Piedmont should draw up a restoration plan.[10]

This report, which touched on most of the key areas of the Piedmontese heritage that are still problematic today, showed how this allocation was viewed as a sort of compensation for the attention being focused on the future, and on technology and industry, which characterised the celebrations of Italia '61. It was to redress the balance with regard to the history of Italy and the buildings in which it had taken shape. A broad and non-literal interpretation of the concept of "Castelli storici del Piemonte" ⁄ the historic castles of Piedmont ⁄ was used in Turin to refer precisely to the masterpieces of the Baroque: Palazzo Reale (fig. 6), Palazzo Chiablese, Palazzo Madama, Castello del Valentino, Villa della Regina. Outside Turin, it included the palace at Stupinigi, the castle of Agliè, Venaria Reale and other buildings not directly related to the age of the Baroque. The funds appeared to be substantial, and yet though they were "[...] apparently considerable, it should be realised that to give definitive

6. Turin, Palazzo Reale. The main facade.

shape solely to the castle of Venaria Reale, which was literally plundered and half destroyed by local vandals after the war, it would be necessary to earmark half of the entire amount available".[11] On the other hand, the scheme was immense and required priorities to be set. It was decided to start work on the most urgent projects, viewing the funds as the start of a grand operation to save the buildings. Despite these limitations and the extreme urgency and the speed ∕ barely two years ∕ with which the task was carried out under the supervision of superintendent Umberto Chieri∕ci, the overall result was one Marziano Bernardi could be proud of.

> Never before had such an undertaking been attempted and carried out to stop the decay of the monuments in Piedmont, and certainly none had ever been carried out so systematically and with such care. The results were cer∕tainly some of the most positive aspects of the celebrations for the centenary of the Unification of Italy...[12]

Even so, this extraordinary event did not usher in the long∕awaited pe∕riod of care for the historical and architectural legacy as a resource that would form part of an economic development project. The development that did take place as a result of the industrial boom, with its turmoil and huge impact on the urban and social fabric, the wave of immigration and the rapid expansion of the suburbs relegated interest in the historical and architectural heritage simply to experts and university circles. In the face of the pressing need to build houses, schools and infrastructure, and the economic expansion driven by industrial growth, the mere idea of devel∕opment partly based on culture and the cultural heritage would have ap∕peared extravagant. In spite of the formidable task of defence carried out in those years by the superintendencies and the continuing work of schol∕ars, it was only in the second half of the 1970s that culture once again came to the fore as an essential component of the quality of life in the met∕ropolitan area. The performing arts were reborn with the institution of many new festivals (one need only think of "Settembre Musica" and the "Punti Verdi" in Turin), while museums and monuments were once again the focus of public interest. The regional government, which had just been created, proved to be very active and the president of the coun∕cil, Aldo Viglione, felt the need for the government to take a leading role, also in symbolic terms, taking up the historic policy of territorial plan∕

7. Rivoli Castle. Entrance to the Museum of Contemporary Art after Andrea Bruno's intervention.

ning started by the Savoys. This led to its interest in the castle of Rivoli and the castle and estate of the Mandria. According to a revealing anecdote, at the end of long negotiations which were very favourable for the heirs of the Medici del Vascello family for the purchase of the Mandria, president Viglione granted the last marquis the right to hunt on his former estate for life. An authentic privilege granted by the king to his vassals. It was however to be paid for, with special rates for deer, wild boar, quails and pheasants, because the regional government had to safeguard public property more than private privileges.

These purchases, which also included other castles in the region and the work to install wine cellars and shops in some of them, were made possible by a certain amount of money provided by the State. There was also a need to give a role to the young institution, which was set up in 1976 with the declared intention of recomposing the historical heritage of the region and putting it to uses that would help develop it. The plan adopted by the regional council in the early 1980s and by Giovanni Ferrero, the councillor for Culture, was to invest in those unique elements that could best enable Piedmont and Turin to distinguish themselves from other cities and areas of art. The idea was to create a solid identity, precisely because investment in culture and cultural heritage was seen as a driving force behind economic development. The Baroque became the ideal candidate as a result of its quantity and extent, and for the way it dominated the territory. This was when the term "Savoy Residences" was coined to indicate the territorial system that included the Crown of Delights and other Savoy residences. It was also possible to integrate and connect it with the system of parks and reserves around the Sacri Monti (Holy Hills).

The most important test bed for all this was to be Rivoli castle, granted on free loan to the regional council after there had been a plan in the 1960s to demolish it since it had been impossible for the local authority to pay for its upkeep. There were symbolic implications behind this: the first royal palace outside Turin, it had been one of the nodes along the Superga-Palazzo Reale-Corso Francia axis, and the fulcrum of the new Capitol dreamed of by Vittorio Amedeo II. A further challenge in the creation of a new and innovative identity, it was decided to include a Museum of Contemporary Art (figs. 7-8) in the restoration of the palace,

8. Rivoli Castle. The west front with the projecting viewing platform.

with an initial plan to house the important collection of American Pop Art amassed by Giuseppe Panza di Biumo. This was a difficult choice, and not without controversy, but tenaciously upheld even after the failure of the negotiations which resulted in its transfer to MOCA in Los Angeles. During the final phases of the restoration project by Andrea Bruno, who had carried out a whole series of studies on the palace in Rivoli when trying to include it in the list of sites to be restored in 1961, the art director of the new museum was Rudi Fuchs, who had been chosen from the group he formed with Pontus Hulten and Harald Szeemann. Upon the suggestion of publisher Umberto Allemandi, he brought together a number of artists of international fame to set up the first exhibition, *Ouverture*, with works and installations designed on site. The restored galleries were transformed into a workshop where Zorio, Merz, Baumgartner, Vedova, Anselma, Sol LeWitt and Long, to name but a few of the most famous, all worked together. With a significant presence of private citizens in the association to assist the activities of the museum, even today the

9. Rivoli Castle. The 'Manica Lunga' and lawn with the restaurant building.

management system remains one of the few experiments that combine public and private control (fig. 9).

The strategy of investing in cultural heritage made another important step forward in the mid 1980s with the concession of Fondi FIO (investment funds for employment). These were designed to promote cultural assets and economic development: over 130 billion lire was invested in important restoration projects in Piedmont during the decade that followed.

Partly as a result of the debate and the achievements of these initiatives, large sections of the public, and no longer simply the experts, gradually became involved. Investments in culture, which were studied and assessed by economists, began to be seen as more than just marginal luxu-

10. Venaria. Aerial view of the village and the royal palace.

ries for a small elite. The Fondazione Giovanni Agnelli financed an important cycle of surveys and studies of the economics of culture and the role of cultural assets in economic development. Meanwhile, restoration work went on at the Castello del Valentino and at the Palazzina di Caccia in Stupinigi, while a plan gradually began to take shape to complete the Crown of Delights with Agliè and Racconigi in a metropolitan museum system.

In December 1996 came the start of the quest to restore Venaria, and in 1999 the European Union approved the feasibility plan, with 120 billion lire made available through structural funds for declining industrial areas. It recognised the contribution that would be made to economic development by the cultural activities which were to take place in the restored building. Funded not only by the European Union but also by the State through lottery funds, the Piedmont Region, the Province of Turin, the local authorities, Fondazione Compagnia di San Paolo and Fondazione CRT, as well as through the Framework Programme Agreements, the Venaria-La Mandria complex (figs. 10-12) became the largest restoration site in Europe. It remains as a symbol of an extraordinary pe-

11. Venaria. Aerial view of the royal palace complex looking towards the village.

12. Venaria, royal palace. Gallery of Diana after restoration in 2005.

riod of investments in cultural resources and museums with a high level of cooperation between the institutions, overcoming the political differences between the City and the Region.

Despite scepticism and criticism, culture and cultural resources became strategic priorities from the mid 1990s, and this remained true also when different governments were voted into office. In 1997 the Savoy Residences became UNESCO World Heritage Sites, as did the Sacri Monti in 2003.

The effects of this policy soon became clear: a massive legacy was returned to the community, and about twenty museums ⁄ some reopened, others new or restored ⁄ joined the metropolitan system within the space of ten years. The monumental staircase of Palazzo Madama has been restored and the entire building itself with the Museo d'Arte Antica will soon be open to the public again. The facades of the Castello del Valentino (fig. 13) have been restored, as has Palazzo Reale, and Villa della Regina (fig. 14) has been reopened. Fifty million euros have been set aside for renovating the Egyptian Museum and the Collegio dei Nobili and countless churches and museums have reacquired their original splendour. These are just some of the steps in this process, and refer only to Baroque buildings. Meanwhile, the number of visitors to museums has

13. Turin, Castello del Valentino. Front on the *cour d'honneur* after the facade was restored in 2005.

14. Turin, Villa della Regina. Main facade of Vitozzi's villa after recent restoration.

quadrupled, from just over 600,000 visitors in 1993 to 2.4 million in 2005.[13] Greater sensitivity to cultural resources has been clearly revealed by a number of pointers, such as the rapid growth in the number of season tickets and museum entrance cards, and the success of the "Rivelazioni Barocche" guided tours programme,[14] as well as by monitoring expectations in post-Olympic Turin,[15] which reveal how the aspects Turin needs to concentrate on for tourism are its museums and the Baroque, which account for 99% and 97% respectively in the preferences of a sample of city residents. They are followed by promotion, nature, food and wine, and accommodation facilities.

These are significant results, due especially to the Olympic events and the greater availability of funds for investments. These funds, which are also regularly provided by bank foundations, make about 70 million euros available for the art and culture sector every year, integrating the investment policy of public authorities. Nevertheless, the most important results will only be seen in the long term: Venaria (where the Restoration Centre is already active, and where much has been completed) still has to consolidate its attraction with a wider public, while the Mandria complex with the Centro del Paesaggio, or 'countryside centre', and the entirety of the Crown of Delights and of the Savoy Residences still has to emerge as a systematic image. The gardens of the various residences contribute significantly to this design, and could well become the first nucleus of a visitor circuit while the restoration of the buildings is being completed. In a world of reduced public funding, the next round of investments needs to complete the strategic centres that will make it possible to open the Residences circuit. One of the most important tasks is to demonstrate a real ability to bring about cultural and economic development, with the promotion of cultural heritage as a decisive and strategic priority.

[1] See B. SECCHI, *La città del ventesimo secolo*, Laterza, Rome-Bari 2000, p. 3.

[2] On this subject, see the studies carried out by Vera Comoli Mandracci, and in particular V. COMOLI MANDRACCI, *Torino*, "Le città nella storia d'Italia" series, Laterza, Rome-Bari 1983 (6th edition 2006).

[3] See G. BOTERO, "Relazione di Piamonte", in G. D. TARINO, *I capitani*, Turin 1607, quoted in V. COMOLI MANDRACCI, *Torino*, "Le città nella storia d'Italia" series, Laterza, Rome-Bari 1983 (6th edition 2006).

[4] See V. COMOLI MANDRACCI, "L'urbanistica della città capitale e del territorio", in G. RICUPERATI (ed.), *Storia di Torino*, vol. IV, *La città fra crisi e ripresa (1630-1730)*, Einaudi, Turin 1998, p. 454.

[5] See A. GRISERI, "Nuovi programmi per le tecniche e la diffusione delle immagini", in G. RICUPERATI (ed.), *Storia di Torino*, vol. III, *Dalla Dominazione francese alla ricomposizione dello Stato (1536-1630)*, Einaudi, Turin 1998, p. 311.

[6] See G. DARDANELLO, "Filippo Juvarra: 'chi poco vede niente pensa'", in G. DARDANELLO (ed.), *Sperimentare l'Architettura. Guarini, Juvarra, Alfieri, Borra e Vittone*, Fondazione CRT, Turin 2001.

[7] Ibid., p. 111.

[8] Ibid.

[9] C. N. COCHIN, *Voyage d'Italie, ou Recueil de Notes sur le ouvrage de Peinture et Sculpture, qu'on voit dans le principales villes d'Italie*, 3 vols., Ch. Ant. Jombert, Paris 1758.

[10] See M. BERNARDI, "Salvezza e restauro dei monumenti Piemontesi", in *La celebrazione del primo centenario dell'Unità d'Italia*, Comitato Nazionale per la Celebrazione del Primo Centenario dell'Unità d'Italia, Turin 1961, p. 601.

[11] Ibid., p. 604.

[12] Ibid., p. 608.

[13] Source: *Osservatorio Culturale del Piemonte*.

[14] Museum season tickets and "Rivelazioni Barocche" are run by the Associazione Torino Città Capitale Europea.

[15] Provincia di Torino, *Le aspettative post-olimpiche nelle Valli olimpiche. Indagine*, April 2006, summary report by Sergio Scamuzzi, Università di Torino - OMERO, Gianluca Bo, Metis Ricerche.

The Baroque and the contemporary world

MICHELA BENENTE

With its heritage of Baroque architecture, which has in many instances
been transformed, the Savoy capital offers an interesting area for research-
ing and analysing the multiple design approaches and logic behind the
various interventions. Often the result of incidental reasons, these attitudes are however important when assessing the relationship that, over
the centuries, contemporary society has had for existing assets. The work
of introducing innovative components into the way buildings are used -
thus rewriting some aspects of Baroque architecture from a contemporary
point of view - needs to be seen in this light. This is true of the royal palace,
Palazzo Reale, which at the time of Carlo Alberto (1835-1845) underwent significant modifications, not just of a functional nature, with the
introduction of bathrooms and lighting and heating installations, but also with renovation of the interiors. The arrangement of the rooms, which

15. Turin, Palazzo Reale. The railings by Pelagio Palagi after restoration in 2005.

were subject also to structural and decorative renovation, was modified to a design by Pelagio Palagi. Palagi took the same approach to the exterior of the royal palace with the creation of the new Dioscuri railings (1835-1839) (figs. 15-16). These railings were placed in front of the palace in the area formerly occupied by the "*pavaglione*", used for the ostension of the Holy Shroud. Built in the early eighteenth century, this pavilion revealed its contemporaneity both in the use of materials and in the inclusion of a lighting system, but it was partly destroyed by fire in 1811. It should be pointed out that the changes made to Palazzo Reale certainly came as a result of the way it was used but, more than anything, it demonstrated a wish to create a symbolic programme for the new king: "Carlo Alberto's national aspirations can be seen in the iconographic programme of a number of works carried out by Palagi".[1]

The attitude of these operations towards the existing Baroque is thus one of total repudiation of its historic and cultural value through the replacement of furnishings, decorations and structures in the palace. This

was pointed out by John Ruskin who, in a quick comment, noted how the splendour of this palace - all that is most graceful - dates back to the time of Louis XIV. The modern part, without exception, shows a total lack of understanding and sensitivity even as regards its splendour: it is totally devoid of dignity and beauty.[2]

The opinion of this English conservative may sound excessive with regard to Palagi's work on Palazzo Reale, but it crops up regularly with regard to many works of the Baroque period. The inclusion of innovative elements in the historical legacy tends to elicit immediate

16. Turin, Palazzo Reale. Detail.

outcry and criticism, but it should nevertheless be pointed out how the historical context of some works can highlight their identity and value.

17. Rivoli, Castle. The end of the Manica Lunga after Andrea Bruno's renovation.

18. Turin, Palazzo Carignano.
The join between Guarini's building
and the 19th-century enlargement.

19. Turin, Palazzo Carignano.
Detail of the courtyard showing the join
between Guarini's 16th-century building
and the 19th-century enlargement.

This is true of the Castello di Rivoli (fig. 17), which is a significant example of how the pre-existing Baroque has acquired new dignity, especially through the use of innovative elements. This is especially true of the
arrangement of the atrium and in the Manica Lunga, or "Long Sleeve",
and in the way "in the Savoy palace, which has survived the events of its
own history, the past is now welded to the present."[3]

   A further example of the juxtaposing of interventions from different eras
can be seen in Palazzo Carignano, where the original structure by Guarini (1679) is mirrored by the nineteenth-century enlargement (1864). The
latter, which was made to house the chamber of the Italian Parliament, is
particularly interesting in the way it seeks to continue the previous architecture (figs. 18-19). The continuation of Guarini's building is obtained
by maintaining the compositional rhythm, the decorative design, and the
same type of construction materials. It should however be pointed out that
the new work can be distinguished by its simplification of the decorative
devices and the use of clearly contemporary materials. The clear distinc-

20. Turin, Palazzo Carignano. Eclectic facade by Giovanni Bollati
(1864-1871) to a design by Domenico Ferri.

tion between the two works is emphasised by the facade that gives onto
Piazza Carlo Alberto, which displays the characteristic eclecticism of the
nineteenth century (fig. 20). On the other hand, it is worth noting how
mid-nineteenth-century opinion about Guarini's work, particularly in
the words of Alfredo d'Andrade,[4] was extremely negative.

There was a similarly indifferent attitude in the late nineteenth and ear-

21. Turin, Collegio dei Nobili. Facade on Piazza Carignano.

ly twentieth century towards the Collegio dei Nobili (fig. 21), which at
the end of the nineteenth century was subjected to a radical division of
the interiors when it was rearranged to house the museums of Egyptian
and Classical Antiquities, of the Natural Sciences, and the Galleria
Sabauda. This transformation eventually led Piero Sanpaolesi in the mid
twentieth century to take out the original structures on the second floor,

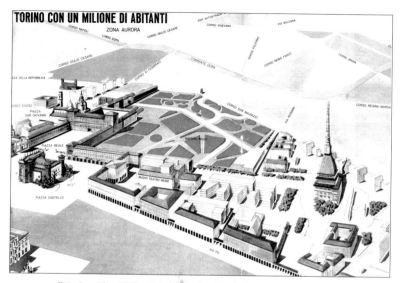

22. "Turin with a Million Inhabitants", a detail of the view of the proposed transformation of the city, in *Tempo*, no. 14, 7 April 1955.

23. Turin, view of the Porte Palatine (Roman gates) following the city transformation project in anticipation of reaching a million inhabitants, in *Tempo*, no. 14, 7 April 1955.

dividing it in two in order to double the exhibition space. In this case, the old building was considered as "no more than a shell, in which it is enough to respect the facades in order to modify the interior at will".[5]

The characteristics of Baroque town-planning and architecture were again disregarded in some large-scale urban projects proposed after the last war, in which the historic fabric of big areas was replaced. One example of this is the "*zona di comando*", or "command zone", which was completely cleared in order to make way for buildings in the International Style, and the introduction of blocks of buildings alongside the archaeological area, which in no way relate to the existing historic and urban setting (figs. 22-23).

From the 1980s, greater attention was paid to renovation and redevelopment plans not only in the case of individual buildings, but for entire areas of the city. For example, the following stand out among the various interventions also effected on parts of the not strictly Baroque layout: the work carried out by Mario Federico Roggero and Agostino Magnaghi in the former convent of Santa Croce; the intervention, again by Roggero, in the former San Giovanni Battista hospital; Giorgio and

24. Turin, Villa della Regina. Detail of the Nymphaeum of the belvedere in the garden.

Giuseppe Raineri's work at the Archivio di Stato; Roberto Gabetti and Aimaro Isola in the Santa Chiara block; and Laura Levi Petrazzini, Roberto Pagliero and Stefano Trucco's work on Filippo Juvarra's Archivio di Corte.

Recent interventions on gardens, however, are more difficult to interpret. An essential ornament for Baroque residences throughout Europe, but inherently fragile and perishable, gardens – especially in Piedmont – were abandoned and then, in recent years, became the object of large-scale restoration operations, or rather of historical revisitation. The most important of these in chronological terms is the garden of Villa della Regina (fig. 24), which had long been subject to improper use and neglect. Its state of decay made it necessary to restore a clear image of the overall design of the garden simply by re-establishing its geometry, though it does still contain some plants from the original arrangement by Ascanio Vitozzi.

The operations planned and completed for the gardens of the royal palace at Venaria are however of greater complexity (figs. 25-26). Here, abandonment and consequent deterioration meant that the historic memory of the garden had been totally compromised. The project report highlights that "all the fragments of the former scenic design are being recomposed" and the garden "is being recovered according to the principle of reusing the place while respecting the signs of its memory, with the awareness that a new and modern entity is being formed."[6]

Lastly, it is worth mentioning those works that have been carried out solely to reconstruct, complete or add in stylistic terms. Examples include the nineteenth-century work on the Castello del Valentino which, when looking at the *Theatrum Sabaudiae* (fig. 27), aimed to propose its ideal completion. The project that Giovanni Vico hoped to carry out was designed to

rejuvenate a work that had become dilapidated and clothe it in a light of its own. This is one of the better results which, it could be said, constitute a very particular art: when reconstructing and terminating a building from another age, every possible effort is made to maintain the distinguishing signs of its era.[7]

25. Venaria, royal palace. Aerial view of the gardens after their recent reconstruction.

26. Venaria, royal palace. View of the royal palace from the fishpond after renovation concluded in 2005.

The modifications made to Domenico Ferri's design (1858) involved the refurbishment of part of the interior decorations and the construction of two wings to replace the seventeenth-century porticoed galleries (fig. 28). The latter take up the style of the earlier building

by continuing the external decorative elements. The facades of the wings, which were widened and raised by one floor, were designed with large windows alternating with small, and the tympanum motifs were repeated modularly, as were the shells and the pilaster strips which framed the windows on the main building.[8]

Baroque architecture was again taken up stylistically in the terraced wings (1864-1867), which were built in place of the hemicycle that closed the courtyard, and in the new wing running parallel to the Po in the direction of Moncalieri (1868-1880).

Similar work was carried out in the completion of the church of San Carlo (fig. 29), in the square of the same name. Begun in 1619, it was completed in the nineteenth century, to a plan that was based "intention-

27. Gio Battista Borgonio, View of the Castello del Valentino illustrating the grandiose, never-completed project, in *Theatrum Sabaudiae*, 1682.

28. Turin, Castello del Valentino. Detail of one of the 19th-century wings.

29. Turin, Piazza San Carlo. View of the 'twin' churches of San Carlo on the right (facade by Ferdinando Caronesi, 1834) and Santa Cristina on the left (facade by Filippo Juvarra, 1715-1718).

ally on Juvarra's design for the facade of the nearby church of Santa Cristina, according to the guidelines provided by the Corpo Decurionale (1834). The rhythm of the front, which is crowned by a broken tympanum, is given by two superimposed orders of columns and composite pilasters."[9] A further interpretation in stylistic terms can be seen in the work of Carlo Ceppi on the pediment that crowns Palazzo Carignano (fig. 30). In 1895 Ceppi also remodelled the church of San Tommaso in Via Pietro Micca in the neo-Baroque style.

The convergence of Baroque and contemporary architecture that occurred in the building of the new Teatro Regio by Carlo Mollino and Marcello Zavellani Rossi (1965-1973) is one of the most evident examples. Of the previous Baroque theatre, which was built from 1738 to a design by Benedetto Alfieri and destroyed by fire in 1936, only the facade that gives onto Piazza Castello remains. The considerable constraints imposed by the uniform design of the square meant that what was still standing should be maintained, while the missing parts should be completed in the same style. Materials similar to the original ones were used, though differently, and can be clearly distinguished. The new design adopted the

30. Turin, Palazzo Carignano. Detail of the gable added by Carlo Ceppi to Guarini's facade.

existing elements as a sort of curtain behind which the new building was to be made (fig. 31). It is worth noticing how the link to the Baroque architecture takes place in the entrance area, which acts as an authentic filter between ancient and modern (fig. 32). Here the use of similar materials differentiated by their surface treatment (polished stone) and the inclusion of glass in-fills in the internal perforations of the Alfieri facade (fig. 33) mark a first step towards the imposing ar-chitecture in glass, metal and ma-sonry of the theatre itself.

The relationship between the centre of Turin and contemporane-

31. Turin, Teatro Regio.
Linking the new theatre to Alfieri's facade.

32. Turin, Teatro Regio. Entrance atrium.

33. Turin, Teatro Regio.
Detail of Alfieri's facade after Carlo
Mollino's intervention.

ity has however taken a number of forms. The presence of the astronomical observatory from 1890 to 1991 at the top of the two towers opposite Juvarra's Palazzo Madama facade is worthy of mention, as is the building of the Torre Littoria (fig. 34). This 'lictorian tower' burst onto the traditional urban landscape, provoking harsh criticism ever since it was built in 1932, for it is seen as "an aggressive sign of urban renewal, not alien to twentieth-century culture",[10] but certainly disruptive of the historic context in which it is placed.

Baroque and contemporary architecture also come together in some temporary installations set up in the grandest squares of Turin. These include those in Piazza Castello, which has been transformed into a flower garden, a skating rink and, more recently, into a huge stage for the Olympic events. The imposing structure set up by Italo Rota in the square transformed the heart of the capital of Savoy into the Olympic Medals Plaza (fig. 35), using mirror-finish surfaces to reflect the architecture of the seventeenth-century facades and create a new image with a kaleidoscope effect. A similarly sharp contrast between expressions of modernity and Baroque urban spaces took place in 1936, when a temporary pavilion in Piazza San Carlo reflected the architectural setting of Castallamonte's facades (fig. 36).

Even though these examples were chapters that came to an end, it should not be forgotten how, in some cases, the creation of temporary constructions in historical contexts can provide an opportunity for creating elements that can remain over the years. This is true of the pavilion designed by Roberto Gabetti and Aimaro Isola to house the facilities to let people with disabilities access the cathedral. It was originally required for the ostension of the Holy Shroud in 1999, but it remained for the Jubilee

34. Turin, Torre Littoria. The tower block built between 1931 and 1932 to a design by Armando Melis de Villa and Giovanni Bernocco.

35. Turin, Piazza Castello. The Medals Plaza,
an installation by Italo Rota for the Winter Olympic
Games in 2006.

36. Turin, pavilion in Piazza San Carlo
for the temporary accommodation of commercial
enterprises in Via Roma, to a design
by Enrico Bonicelli.

37. Turin, service pavilion for access to the Cathedral, built to a design by Roberto Gabetti and Aimaro Isola.

the following year and it is still being used today. The pavilion, which was built next to the cathedral, is placed up against the side facade of Palazzo Reale. Working next to existing architecture obliges architects to reflect on how their designs fit in, and how their solutions tend not towards mimicry but, on the contrary, towards finding an efficient way of inserting their work into the context, without causing noticeable rifts with the past (fig. 37).

[1] See A. M. MATTEUCCI, "Scenografia e architettura nell'opera di Pelagio Palagi", in *Pelagio Palagi artista e collezionista*, exhibition catalogue (Bologna, April-September 1976), Grafis, Bologna 1976, p. 116.

[2] See P. M. PROSIO, *Guida letteraria di Torino*, Centro Studi Piemontesi, Turin 1993, p. 31.

[3] See G. ROMANO, "Presentazione", in A. BRUNO, *Il Castello di Rivoli. 1734-1984 storia di un recupero*, Allemandi, Turin 1984, p. 11. Andrea Bruno's work has been much criticised, with harsh observations expressed by Pierre-Alain Croset in P. A. CROSET, "Architetture in Piemonte 1980-1989", in P. A. CROSET (ed.), *Architetture degli anni '80 in Piemonte*, Electa, Milan 1990, pp. 36-37.

[4] See the words quoted by C. PALMAS, "Dal salone Guariniano all'Aula del parlamento Subalpino (1682-1848)", in *Il Parlamento Subalpino in Palazzo Carignano strutture e restauro*, Utet, Turin 1988, p. 43.

[5] See S. CURTO, *Storia del Museo Egizio di Torino*, Centro Studi Piemontesi, Turin 1976, p. 16.

[6] See F. PERNICE, *I Giardini della Reggia de La Venaria Reale*, in F. PERNICE (ed.), *La Venaria Reale. Lavori a corte*, Progetto La Venaria Reale, Turin 2003, p. 67.

[7] See G. VICO, *Il Real Castello del Valentino, Monografia Storica*, Reale Stamperia, Turin 1858, p. 59.

[8] See C. ROGGERO BARDELLI, "Il Valentino", in C. ROGGERO BARDELLI, M. G. VINARDI and V. DEFABIANI, *Ville Sabaude*, Rusconi, Milan 1990, p. 207.

[9] See V. COMOLI MANDRACCI and P. SCARZELLA (eds.), "Quartiere 1. Centro", in V. COMOLI MANDRACCI (ed.), *Beni culturali ambientali nel Comune di Torino*, Società degli Ingegneri e degli Architetti in Torino, Turin 1984, 2 vols., vol. II, entry 211, p. 320.

[10] See A. MAGNAGHI, M. MONGE and L. RE, *Guida all'architettura moderna di Torino*, 2nd edition, Celid, Turin 2005, p. 139.

Baroque and restoration

MICHELA BENENTE

The recognition of historical and cultural value is a fundamental prem‑
ise for carrying out any restoration project. Viewed in these terms, it
should be pointed out how, until the mid twentieth century, Baroque ar‑
chitecture was subjected more to normal upkeep and repair than to com‑
prehensive restoration projects. Authentic restoration work was limited
to medieval buildings. One example of this is the work carried out by
Alfredo d'Andrade on Palazzo Madama (1883‑1885),[1] which con‑
cerned only the castle of the princes d'Acaja, and even went so far as to
medievalise parts of the Juvarra extension.

Some distinctions and exceptions do, however, need to be made. These
include the strengthening of the twin columns that form the arcades in

38. Turin, Piazza San Carlo.
Detail of the twin columns of the
arcade after being reinforced by
Benedetto Alfieri.

Piazza San Carlo (fig. 38). The work
was carried out by Benedetto Alfieri as
early as 1753, incorporating them in large
pilasters and filling in the oculi above
with panels containing stucco decora‑
tions. It was therefore exceptional events
that led to work on seventeenth‑ and eigh‑
teenth‑century monuments, and this in‑
cluded damage caused during the Sec‑
ond World War and the destruction of
much of Turin's architectural heritage.
Piazza San Carlo itself was badly hit
during the air raids and, after fierce de‑
bate, it was reconstructed as from 1946
under the supervision of Vittorio Mes‑
turino, superintendent of monuments in
Piedmont (fig. 39). The project called for
the reconstruction of the parts that had

39. Turin, Piazza San Carlo. View of the elevation of Castellamonte's square
after post-war reconstruction and restoration in 2000.

been destroyed and opposed the demolition of what was left in order to
make new buildings. As Mesturino saw it, demolition would have led
to "business speculation rather than safeguarding an architectural heritage of historic and artistic interest".[2] Speculation certainly led to most
of the post-war work on what were supposedly "minor" buildings. Mar-
ginalised in the national debate on conservation right up until the mid
twentieth century, also in Turin they were paid far less attention than the
more important sites.

   On the contrary, the work carried out from 1890 on the courtly halls
of the Castello del Valentino was truly exceptional. While previous intervention had aimed at stylistic completion, on this occasion a full programme of restoration took place. D'Andrade considered that "the fres-
co decoration of the palace hall is a fairly good work of the seventeenth
century and is not only worthy of being restored but also of being held in

higher esteem than has been the case so far",[3] and only the vault was re-inforced. It was not until 1924 that general restoration was carried out, though again in stylistic terms, and some of the decorations in the hall of honour were remodelled.

On the other hand, some reconstruction work which did not exactly recreate the original style took place on the buildings destroyed in Via Po and Piazza Castello during Second World War bombing raids. While "no one in Turin would have admitted that the reconstructed facades giv-ing onto the street departed from the principles behind the old rules of ar-chitectural uniformity",[4] the reconstruction (1951) of the buildings de-signed by Castellamonte in Via Po (fig. 40) respected the height of the cornices and the presence of arcades on the ground floor, but modified the interior divisions and thus the layout of the openings on the fronts. There is also "an inextricable topological contrast with the original al-ternation of the tympana [...], which can be seen in the technologically different solutions for the window frames".[5] Another distinguishing fea-

40. Turin, Via Po. Building reconstructed in the post-war years. The insertion of roll-up shutters is noticeable.

ture of this work is the use of beams and floor slabs in reinforced concrete for the arcades, which nevertheless maintained the same height and rhythm as the seventeenth-century street front (fig. 41).

Similar work was carried out on the bombed buildings in Piazza Castello. Some of the buildings in the Santa Caterina and San Gaetano blocks in the square, which give onto Via Pietro Micca and Via Palazzo di Città, were also destroyed. The two buildings, which had not been raised in height during the nineteenth century, still conformed to the original design by Vitozzi when the war broke out. In the Santa Caterina block, reconstruction work involved the

41. Turin, Via Po. Comparison between Castellamonte's buildings and post-war reconstructions.

42. Turin, Piazza Castello. The Santa Caterina block: post-war reconstruction with the addition of roll-up shutters and reinforced-concrete floor slabs.

43. Turin, Piazza Castello. The Santa Caterina block: front on Piazza Castello.

making of a new building which maintained the original design on the streets (fig. 42), while on the square there was only one arch in place of the original two, which again took up the design of the old front (fig. 43). This operation, which started in 1946, shows how attention was paid only to the outer skin of the building, without giving any importance to the construction as a whole. Reinforced-concrete floor slabs modified the complex, replacing the beams of the previous arcades. The reconstruction of the second building, on the corner of Via Palazzo di Città, was subject to complex procedures that ended in 1969. These were carried out in compliance with the indications provided by the superintendency, which "called for a project faithful to the design and symmetry of the facade" in order to "achieve a level of completeness that was never carried out and a selection of everything that was not consistent with it".[6] The reconstruction was perfectly mimetic, (fig. 44) with even the recreation of the barrel vault in the arcade, though on the Via Palazzo di Città side there was a total violation, clearly contradicting what had been requested by the superintendency for the Piazza Castello front, with a glass facade resting on an arcade with reinforced-concrete columns creating a striking contrast (fig. 45). We can also see how the bombing raids which hit the city and its architectural heritage led to emergency work on the

44. Turin, Piazza Castello. The San Gaetano block: stylistic reconstruction of the front on Piazza Castello.

most important monuments involved. While post-war photographs preserve the memory of the many seventeenth- and eighteenth-century monuments that were damaged - including Palazzo Madama, Palazzo Lascaris, the Carmine and Santa Teresa churches, Castello del Valentino, and Villa della Regina - in actual fact the restoration work carried out on them erased their style through the introduction of new elements. Reconstruction as it was and where it was - which has been accepted more in response to psychological demands than to cultural principles - once again became of great topical interest during the debate on the restoration of the chapel of the Holy Shroud (Cappella della Santa Sindone) (fig. 46).[7]

Even though Baroque architecture is viewed as a fundamental aspect of the city and the region, when one considers its restoration one can see how it has never really been the subject of a coordinated programme covering all its various elements. Seventeenth- and eighteenth-century architecture has indeed been included in many far-reaching programmes involving buildings from other ages, but so far the Baroque as such has never been considered as a single objective for improvement and restoration plans. This can be seen in the works carried out for the various celebratory events that have taken place in the Turin area, from the hundredth anniversary

45. Turin, Piazza Castello. The San Gaetano block: glass facade
on Via Palazzo di Città.

46. Turin, chapel of the Holy Shroud. The chapel enveloped in scaffolding after the fire of 1997.

of the Unification of Italy (1961), through to the G7 summit (1997), the Jubilee (2000), and the Winter Olympic Games (2006). These event-related restoration projects have involved important Baroque buildings and, more recently, squares as well in more complex restoration programmes. For the celebrations of the Unification of Italy, the buildings were chosen for their links with the events of the Risorgimento and for the fact that they were owned by the State - with the result that the palaces of Rivoli and Racconigi, for example, were left untouched. The substantial intervention carried out from 1959 ranged from work to liberate and consolidate the palace in Venaria to replacement and refurbishment operations in Palazzo Reale, as well as the complex works carried out on the Castello del Valentino. In the case of the Valentino palace, paintings and stuccos were restored, superstructures removed and the roofs remade, and the facades were returned to their original splendour. Similar work was carried

47. Turin, archaeological park of the Porte Palatine (Roman gates). The new bastion was built on the foundations of the old one, demolished during the 19th century.

out on Palazzo Madama, where the "disintegration of the Gassino stone" led to the replacement of "capitals, cornices, balustrades, statues and decorative flames".[8]

While the limited economic resources available for the Unification celebrations also led to the spasmodic and frenetic 'rescue' of part of the architectural heritage (there was a period of just two years between the allocation of funds and the unveiling of the works in 1961), the scope of the operations for the 2006 Olympics was far greater. There are however some who see a similarity in the way the need for immediate effects was given greater priority than real preservation of the heritage.[9] In particular, the increased range of operations included works to redevelop, or rather redesign, the image of the city, involving not just individual sites but also urban areas, which have also been the focus of contradictory assessments. One emblematic example is the redevelopment of the area next to the Porte Palatine (fig. 47), recently completed to a design by Aimaro Isola, Giovanni Durbiano and Luca Reinero, which caused fierce debate about the approach to be adopted. On the one hand, Paolo Marconi in *Il Giornale dell'Arte* referred to the work on the archaeological area as the "best restoration of 2005",[10] while Giuseppe Culicchia in *La Stampa* referred to it as a "historical fake" with Las Vegas-style overtones.[11]

48. Turin, church of San Lorenzo.
Guarini's dome seen from the arcades of the Segreterie di Stato.

Controversy also raged around the many works to beautify buildings, streets and squares with the restoration of facades, new paving, street furniture and plants, "with a view to 'reclaiming' an image more with a view to obtaining easy consent rather than respecting the cultural value of the legacy".[12] Apart from the specific results of each intervention, the object of discussion and contrasting opinions, the policy aimed at enhancing public urban spaces had an important effect in restoring previously decayed and ill frequented places to intense and vital public use.

The imposing restoration work carried out for celebratory events - and not just for the Olympics - should not however let us forget what has been achieved in more ordinary times. There has been considerable restoration work since the late 1970s, involving a number of Baroque buildings. These include the churches of San Lorenzo (fig. 48) and Santa Cristina, the Castello di Rivoli and Palazzo Carignano, to mention but a few, as well as the Stupinigi hunting lodge (fig. 49).

Stupinigi, which was restored by Roberto Gabetti and Aimaro Isola with the assistance of Giuseppe Bellezza and Maurizio Momo in the late 1980s, is an important example in terms of the methodology adopted. The work carried out was inspired by Paolo Marconi's *Manuale di recupero*, from the phase based on in-depth knowledge of the structure and the 'work-in-progress' nature of the project. According to Gabetti himself, "restoration is viewed as a technical and operational procedure based on the work being carried out, and not as a complex and predefined process". The Stupinigi site also enabled restoration experts and history of architecture scholars to learn and compare notes, and in 1991 it became the subject of a seminar on specialisation in architectural restoration. The work on the Stupinigi palace was a fundamental watershed also in terms of the restoration of building facades. At Stupinigi, the "'Turin yellow', which local rhetoric had referred to as a particular 'invention of tradition',"[13] was definitively done away with and a range of light colours was adopted on the facade. The operation, which entered the national debate on city colours, paved the way for similar works, including the restoration of the facade of Palazzo Reale.[14]

Lastly, the drafting of joint plans should be mentioned. These include "Residenze e collezioni sabaude" - the "Savoy Residences and Collec-

49. Stupinigi, hunting lodge. View of the main front after restoration by Roberto Gabetti, Aimaro Oreglia d'Isola, Giuseppe Bellezza and Maurizio Momo.

tions" project ⸱ better known as the "Progetto FIO 1982", which started up a period of study and restoration of the Savoy residences and helped lead to their inclusion in the UNESCO World Heritage List. This event gave the Savoy heritage an important opportunity, for inclusion in the list does not merely provide a useful showcase but also gives the opportunity for cultural assets to be included in integrated promotion policies. These policies go beyond the safeguarding, preservation and defence of individual constructions to enhance all the material and immaterial aspects related to them. In particular, the request by UNESCO to draw up special management plans introduced a new way of looking at cultural assets not only as individual elements, which can be included in different combinations as the occasion arises, but also as an ensemble.[15]

[1] See the description by A. TELLUCCINI in *Il Palazzo Madama di Torino*, Lattes, Turin 1928.

[2] See M. MATTONE, *Vittorio Mesturino architetto e restauratore*, Alinea, Florence 2005, p. 53.

[3] The quotation is included in M. DI MACCO, "Progetto e restauro per la riqualificazione delle residenze", in *Il progetto per interventi in edifici antichi, Teoria e Pratica*, proceedings of the seminar on specialisation in architectural restoration (September 1991), Fondazione Palazzina Stupinigi, Turin 1994, p. 143.

[4] See L. RE, "I danni di guerra", in M. G. VINARDI (ed.), *Danni di guerra a Torino. Distruzione e ricostruzione dell'immagine nel centro della città*, Celid, Turin 1997, p. 55.

[5] Ibid., p. 56.

[6] See C. OCCELLI, "Piazza Castello", in M. G. VINARDI (ed.), *Danni di guerra a Torino...* cit., p. 84.

[7] On this subject, see the considerations of scholars and experts concerning the possible solutions to be adopted in *La cappella della Sindone*, Allemandi, Turin 1997, pp. 55-62.

[8] See M. BERNARDI, "Salvezza e restauro dei monumenti piemontesi", in *La celebrazione del primo centenario dell'Unità d'Italia*, Comitato Nazionale per la Celebrazione del Primo Centenario dell'Unità d'Italia, Turin 1961, p. 608.

[9] See M. A. GIUSTI, "Il restauro architettonico", in M. A. GIUSTI (ed.), *Temi di restauro*, Celid, Turin 2000, p. 51.

[10] See P. MARCONI, in *Il Giornale dell'Arte*, no. 250, January 2006, p. 30.

[11] See G. CULICCHIA, "L'architetto del nostro futuro? È Walt Disney", in *La Stampa*, 15 February 2006, p. 36.

[12] See E. ROMEO, "Torino, le piazze storiche", in *Parametro*, no. 239, May-June 2002, p. 63.

[13] R. GABETTI and A. ISOLA, "Juvarra dopo Juvarra", in R. GABETTI and A. GRISERI (eds.), *Stupinigi. Luogo d'Europa*, Allemandi, Turin 1996, p. 15.

[14] See D. BIANCOLINI (ed.) "La quinta di facciata dei palazzi e ville reali, riflessioni e testimonianze di storia e restauro", in *I giornali di restauro*, no. 2, Celid, Turin 1994.

[15] On this subject, see T. K. KIROVA, "Problematiche di attuazione della Convenzione del Patrimonio Mondiale. Monitoraggio e rapporto periodico, sperimentazione in alcuni casi pilota: Barumini, San Gimignano, Val di Noto", in P. MICOLI and M. R. PALOMBI (eds.), *I siti italiani iscritti nella Lista del Patrimonio Mondiale dell'UNESCO: esperienze e potenzialità*, Diffusioni grafiche, Alessandria 2004, pp. 71-97 and T. K. KIROVA, "Il processo di conoscenza e di valorizzazione per la gestione dei siti italiani UNESCO", in P. MICOLI and M. R. PALOMBI (eds.), *I siti italiani iscritti nella Lista del Patrimonio Mondiale dell'UNESCO. Piano di gestione e rapporto periodico*, Diffusioni grafiche, Alessandria 2005, pp. 52-65.

Baroque issues
LUCA DAL POZZOLO

A VAST ENTERPRISE

The size of the Baroque heritage that has come down to us is so vast ⁄ even for the Crown of Delights alone ⁄ that the question of economic sustain⁄ ability simply cannot be ignored. It must be said that, quite apart from the preferences of the various monarchs who at times might choose Ve⁄ naria, at others Stupinigi or Racconigi, the unfinished buildings, the abandoned building sites, and the long periods of neglect themselves cre⁄ ated a historic problem of economic sustainability which has come down to us in its entirety. The enormous joint effort by the regional, national and provincial governments, local authorities, the Fondazione San Pao⁄ lo and the Fondazione CRT, partly regulated by Framework Programme Agreements and with a sizeable contribution from the European Union, which has been a feature of policies regarding the restoration of cultural resources and museums over the past ten years, amounts to something like 800⁄1000 million euros. Even so, the work still remains to be completed and the Savoy Residences circuit still needs massive investments for restoration so that it can be fully opened to the public.

An emblematic symbol of this is Venaria: the cost of restoration and extra infrastructure is estimated at over 250 million euros, covering more than 50,000 square metres of floor space, together with more than 30,000 at La Mandria, 120 hectares of garden, miles of museum tours and visits to be prepared ⁄ and the list of records could continue. These are historic records, which even at the time were extraordinary, as in the case of the failed project to build Juvarra's immense "Citronnière", or orangery.

Havendo noi preso l'impresa di far una Scuderia, e Citronera, ci hanno fatto fare una Fabrica d'una alzata straordinaria, e tutta ornamenti, cioè zoccoli, riquadri, circolari, ovali, nicchie, e piombature, che trà tutte compongono il tutto. Fabbrica più tosto di un magnifico tempio, che d'una Scuderia, e Citronera, e se c'havessero mostrato il disseg⁄ no, come si doveva, dell'alzata, et ornamenti nel deliberm.o non si sarebbe ne meno fat⁄

50. Venaria, royal palace. Restoration of the Citronnière.

ta d.a Fab.a a £50 cad. Trab. E massime che in questo Paese le Citronere sono Crotte, et nell'instrutione si dice che sopra detta Citronera si faranno l'abitationi per li domes-tici, il che ci ha fatto creder una Fabbrica ordinaria ["After we had undertaken the task of making the Stables, and a Citronnière, they had us construct a build-ing of extraordinary height, adorned throughout, with plinths, frames, cir-cles, ovals, niches, and lead-work, which all together form the whole. An edifice more similar to a magnificent temple than to a stables and a citron-nière, and if, as they should have done, they had shown us that drawing of the height, and of the ornaments, in the resolution, said edifice would not have been made even for £50 each. And in this country citronnières are ul-timately caverns, and the instructions indicated that above said citronnière there would be the dwellings of the servants, which made us think it would be an ordinary building.]¹

The need to find integrated and compatible roles for Venaria (fig. 50) and to create an entire area capable of attracting a million visitors a year - as provided for in the budget on which the European Union funding is based ⁄ has been a challenge for the various projects that have been pro⁄ posed. The idea of moving the Egyptian Museum to the Citronnière di⁄ vided intellectuals, experts in the cultural sector, and public opinion, but it has now been shelved. Eight years have gone by since work started and many parts have already been completed (the church of Sant'Uberto, the Galleria di Diana and the museum visit, which is being set up, the Reg⁄ gia di Diana, most of the gardens, and the Restoration Centre which is now up and running), while others are being terminated (the Citron⁄ nière and the Stables, the second floors, and so on). Now has come the time to experiment the management systems and to open up this immense Baroque leisure machine to see how it works. It cannot be compared with a museum or a single cultural venue, for it is the size of an immense theme park, with all the problems and challenges that that entails.

THE CIRCUIT OF THE RESIDENCES AND THE LAYOUT OF THE TERRITORY

As well as restoring the individual buildings, the Savoy Residences and the smaller circuit around Turin ⁄ the so⁄called Crown of Delights de⁄ signed by Castellamonte ⁄ formed a system for organising and control⁄ ling the territory. It included a web of roads and infrastructures that to⁄ gether implemented its absolutist plan. In particular, the semicircle on which the Crown of Delights is based was designed so that it could be covered on horseback in one day, with the residences acting as resting places at almost regular intervals. This territorial layout has now been submerged by the urban development which brushes up against and en⁄ ters into contact with the various residences, and the circular links of the Crown around Turin have now been replaced by the motorway ring road. Today the issue is to restore what will become a future landscape corridor along which visitors will be able to travel at ease, in pleasant sur⁄ roundings, without being forced to accompany their enjoyment of a De⁄ light with long periods of transit through down⁄at⁄heel suburbs. On the other hand, even with such massive investments for restoring the Savoy Residences, the fact that the new Metro system stops in Collegno, more than seven kilometres from Rivoli, and the tram two kilometres from Stupinigi, give an idea of the difficulties involved in managing the sys⁄

tem and its infrastructures at the metropolitan level. Ironically, when the Castello di Rivoli was being restored, there was a well-founded fear that it would not be finished before the Metro arrived: twenty years later, the palace still suffers from the now almost historic difficulty of access by public transport.

And yet it is precisely the opening of the circuit - at least that of the Crown of Delights with Agliè and Racconigi - that creates the potential for giving international credence to this extraordinary complex of cultural assets and to ensure the economic viability of its management with a consistent influx of visitors. Twenty-five years after the first restoration of the palace and the park, Racconigi now has a full programme of activities (even without the presence of the circuit) and has become the most visited cultural venue outside Turin. About 200,000 visitors are expected in 2006, showing what enormous potential the circuit will have when it is complete. By making the right organisational effort, this circuit could be opened right now: not all the interiors of the palaces could be visited, but the stunning array of parks and gardens, of all types and of different eras, could be made available. These are treasures that even today arouse keen and popular interest. The important thing is that it must be seen as a complete system, with its roots in the organisation of the territory and with each element as the centre of an extraordinary cultural heritage.

THE CENTRAL DISTRICT OF CULTURE

The centre of Turin, within the area of the eighteenth-century walls, is packed with cultural institutions, including theatres (Regio, Gobetti, Carignano, Auditorium), the headquarters of cultural associations and institutions such as the RAI, universities, libraries, cinemas and nineteen out of the thirty-nine museums in the metropolitan area,[2] most of which are in Baroque buildings. Even so, this district cannot actually be seen as such, for the museums are crammed into their superb architecture, but they lack the necessary space for services and cannot accommodate the public with the level of service required by contemporary standards.

It is thus not possible to benefit from the dual advantage of having a complete and centrally placed cultural district: on the one hand, an urban context and an ability to attract visitors to an international citadel of

51. Turin, Collegio dei Nobili and the church of San Filippo Neri.

52. Turin, Palazzo Carignano. Guarini's facade after restoration in 2005.

culture, and on the other, the possibility of solving problems concerning the need for extra space and expansion within the city, as well as the problems of architectural decay encountered by the individual buildings. By moving the Galleria Sabauda from the Collegio dei Nobili to the new wing of Palazzo Reale means that the Egyptian Museum will be able to expand, and an organic, centrally located museum district can be planned. A lot will depend on what is decided for the Collegio dei Nobili and the way the new Egyptian Museum will be designed. The Olympics and the new arrangements of the sculpture collections, created by Oscar-winning set designer Dante Ferretti, have led to a considerable increase in the number of visitors, which may well exceed half a million a year.

Especially when considering the massive influx of visitors, the suitability of the Collegio dei Nobili for the city's most famous and important museum cannot simply be taken for granted, as the previous work by Sanpaolesi-Gabrielli to fit the Galleria Sabauda into the building demonstrated. The ability of a fragmented, urban facility to absorb an influx of this size or even greater, and to involve the nearby buildings and surrounding city area (including Piazza Carignano, Palazzo Carignano, and San Filippo (figs. 51/52), will show if it is possible for a centrally placed cultural district to emerge and play a leading role in the search for a post/industrial and post/Olympic urban identity.

THE "COMMAND ZONE"

The heart of the central district is undoubtedly the "command zone", which extends with spectacular ramifications from the cathedral almost as far as the shadow of the Mole Antonelliana, taking in Palazzo Reale, the Segreterie di Stato, the Archivio di Stato, the Teatro Regio, the Zec/ca (the former Mint) and the Cavallerizza Reale complex (fig. 53). The uniform appearance of this extraordinary ensemble has been pointed out in a number of in/depth studies.[3]

> The architectural design of the great complex, which can be attributed to Amedeo di Castellamonte, [...] created / as we can still observe, in spite of

53. Turin, aerial photograph of the 'command zone'.

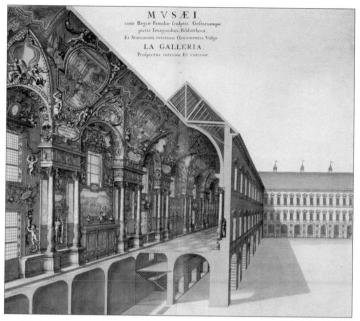

54. Gio Battista Borgonio, perspective view and section of the Gallery of the Royal Armoury, in *Theatrum Sabaudiae*, 1682.

a number of demolitions - a sort of great palace-city, a symbol of the power and magnificence of the dynasty. What we normally refer to as Palazzo Reale was, and indeed still is, simply the courtly hub of the larger complex of "Fabbriche Regie", or "royal edifices", that was created between the sixteenth and the nineteenth centuries, closing the northern side of the city from the Porta Palazzo area to the beginning of Via Po.[4]

It contains the "Polo Reale" project, which aims to rethink the way that the areas and museums in the 'royal zone' are interconnected and used. The complex includes Palazzo Chiablese, the chapel of the Holy Shroud, Palazzo Reale, the royal armoury and the royal library, which are now all separate, but which it would be both interesting and necessary to bring together so that visitors are no longer obliged to keep going in and out of the same building, paying for a new ticket every time (fig. 54).

Even so, one also needs to think on a larger scale, taking in the Segreterie di Stato (the former offices of the Secretary of State, now occupied

55. Turin, Cavallerizza Reale. Entrance from Via Verdi.

56. Turin, Cavallerizza Reale. The Chiablese riding school.

by the Prefecture), the Teatro Regio, the national archives, and all the riding areas and buildings of the Cavallerizza complex, which is a juxtaposition of works by Castellamonte, Baroncelli, Juvarra and Alfieri (figs. 55-56). In the heart of the old town, this immense palace-city, which remains something of a mystery in the minds of the people of Turin, contains more than 50,000 square metres waiting to be put to good use. This makes it a strategic resource of huge importance, placing Turin in the geographical network of Europe's cultural capitals.[5] It is here that a far-reaching project might locate the nerve centre of the central district, re-examining the museum system and integrating all the areas of public use so that the various buildings and the connections between them can be seen as a whole. This would make it possible for the "command zone" to emerge once again embedded in the urban fabric - no longer a phantom district and an urban void in the imagination and everyday life of the city (figs. 57-58). This is a complex project: the extreme fragmentation of the property, the large number of institutions involved, and the size of

57. Turin, Cavallerizza Reale.
View of one of the courtyards,
used as a private car park.

58. Turin, Via Verdi.
Street fronts of the Cavallerizza
and Teatro Regio.

59. Turin, chapel of the Holy Shroud before the fire of 1997.

60. Turin, chapel of the Holy Shroud before the fire of 1997.

the undertaking mean that no simple and rapid solutions are possible. Nevertheless, if the plan is not wide enough in scope, the risk is that these priceless resources ⁄ this city within a city ⁄ will be under⁄utilised as a 'treasure house' of spaces unavailable elsewhere: museum storage space, university lecture rooms, secondary museum headquarters, archives and miscellaneous services that might compromise the closely integrated nature of the entire "command zone" if not included in a clear plan.

THE CHAPEL OF THE HOLY SHROUD

During the night of 11 April 1997 Guarino Guarini's masterpiece caught fire when restoration work had just finished and it was about to be reopened (figs. 59⁄61). Pictures of immense flames shooting out of the oculi, casting sparks and a terrifying orange glow over the cathedral, Palazzo Chiablese and the royal palace, were beamed around the world, causing a wave of emotion. Over the following days, it was not just the cordoned⁄off Piazza San Giovanni that attracted curious onlookers, for the

61. Turin, chapel of the Holy Shroud immediately after the fire of 1997.

numbers of visitors to the museums in the centre of the city also increased ⁄ a phenomenon of micro⁄tourism and attraction induced by the catas⁄ trophe.[6] The fire placed the static quality of the building in serious dan⁄ ger and destroyed all the decorative work on the inside. In spite of the dif⁄ ficulties involved, nine years later the solution required to restore the stat⁄ ic resistance of the dome has been found and is now being put into effect, while complex problems have arisen concerning the approach to be adopted for salvaging and restoring the decoration of the interior. Far from being just an ordinary interior decoration, with wood and painted stuc⁄ coes, it was a sort of thick skin based on stereometrics ⁄ in other words, on the art of the geometrical cutting of stone and ashlar, using building processes and craftsmen's skills of great variety and expertise, Renaissance techniques, and specially designed methods that were introduced and carried out under the supervision of Guarini himself. This is why it was so important to study the feasibility of carrying out an operation to repeat the complex production process that made the chapel of the Holy Shroud so unique, avoiding the use of artificial materials and stucco to recreate

62. Gio Battista Borgonio, bird's eye view of the city, in *Theatrum Sabaudiae*, 1682.

just its superficial appearance. It is important not to create just a surface skin of decoration separate from the underlying structure, losing the close relationship between the geometries, the textures and the materials with their original construction processes, and the technology behind them.

The study is now complete and it is possible to move on to the planning stage, carrying out a restoration and reconstruction that is certainly one of the most complex both in terms of technical and technological problems, and in terms of the expectations and the attention that the results are bound to provoke.

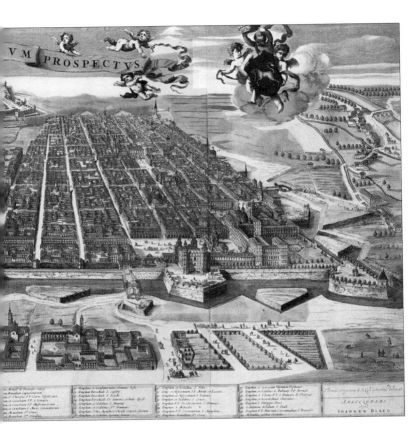

A EUROPEAN VISION AND A HERITAGE
STILL TO BE EXPLOITED

The very reasons for the creation of this Baroque heritage, the training of the architects who devised it, and the policy of grandeur that was behind it were all part of a European vision, and it was for this reason that the *Theatrum Sabaudiae* was produced on such a grand scale. The vastness and the magnificence of the architecture were to give Turin and the Duchy of Savoy its position in the political geography of that age (fig. 62).

Three hundred years later, this is the scale that the enormous effort to give the Baroque heritage its true value once again will have to work on. This is the scale on which the issues of cultural, social and economic sustainability will have to be assessed in order to make Turin and Piedmont one of the capitals and territories of European culture, placing them on the tourist maps and among the cities in which it is a pleasure to live. Places where culture and innovation come together against a variegated backdrop of history, offering not just memories of the past but also a world of discovery, a sense of belonging, and an experiment in imagination. Even though it is important and cannot be neglected, it is not just a matter of cashing in on the advantages of extra tourism, but one of creating a strong identity. The idea is not to compete with other artistic centres in Italy, but to represent the distinctive features of an entire territory in a society that increasingly finds in culture the building blocks it needs for future development. This comprehensive vision thus needs to act as a guideline for the many choices that still need to be made in order to make the most of this historic legacy, avoiding as far as possible an approach based on individual circumstances and needs. All too often our cultural heritage runs the risk of being considered more of a problem than a resource, great buildings as mere containers to be occupied in a sort of never-ending musical chairs, quite divorced from their historic significance and from the way they constitute central nodes in an urban fabric. They are the true ganglions and nerves of a highly complex historical system. It would therefore make no sense today to have these resources ⁄ Baroque and post-Olympic buildings ⁄ compete in a race to put them back in working order and use them again, building by building, site by site. It is not because of any diversity in the dignity of the architecture, but because these works belong to habitats with different significances, with different values and visions, and with equally important but different relationships with the contemporary world.

It is worth pointing out that, together with the many great decisions to be made, there is a large and widespread heritage throughout Piedmont which still needs to be promoted and discovered by the public at large. It is one that is woven into the countryside, in the provincial towns and villages, and it too can be used to put the spotlight on areas of the highest scenic and environmental quality. One need only think of a possible tour of the works by a master of Baroque architecture such as Antonio

Bernardo Vittone, who was in no way of secondary importance, visiting churches and chapels, and entering the dizzy world of a maze-like interweaving of cultural itineraries made possible by the wealth of this land's historic heritage.

[1] Archivio di Stato di Torino, Corte, Palazzi Reali, Venaria Reale, fasc. IV: 1722 in 1728, "Scritture, memorie, esami, ed estimo di periti concernenti le differenze poscia insorte tra l'Intendenza della casa di S.M. e gli impresari Serena, Piazza e Compagnia", in DARDANELLO (ed.) *Sperimentare l'Architettura. Guarini, Juvarra, Alfieri, Borra e Vittone*, Fondazione CRT, Turin 2001, p. 166.
[2] Museo Pietro Micca, Palazzo Reale, Armeria Reale, Museo di Antichità, Museo Nazionale del Risorgimento, Museo Egizio, Galleria Sabauda, Palazzo Bricherasio, Palazzo Barolo, Museo Regionale di Scienze Naturali, Pinacoteca Albertina, Museo della Sindone, Museo Nazionale del Cinema, Fondazione Accorsi, Palazzo Cavour, Biblioteca Reale, Fondazione Teatro Regio, and Palazzo Madama. This list does not include the Galleria d'Arte Moderna, which lies outside the area originally enclosed by the city walls.
[3] See V. COMOLI MANDRACCI (ed.), *Beni culturali ambientali nel Comune di Torino*, Società degli Ingegneri e degli Architetti in Torino, Turin 1984, 2 vols.
[4] P. CORNAGLIA, "Il palazzo diventa città: la Grande Galleria, l'Accademia Reale, il Teatro, la Zecca e la Dogana nell'impianto di Amedeo di Castellamonte", in F. BAGLIANI, P. CORNAGLIA, M. MADERNA and P. MIGHETTO, *Architettura, governo e burocrazia in una capitale barocca. La zona di comando di Torino e il piano di Filippo Juvarra del 1730*, doctorate in the History and Criticism of Architectural and Environmental Resources series, Celid, Turin 2000.
[5] A feasibility study has been carried out by Agostino Magnaghi to examine the development potential of the Cavallerizza.
[6] Source: Osservatorio Culturale del Piemonte.

© 2006 UMBERTO ALLEMANDI & C., TURIN
VIDEOLAYOUT ROSARIO PAVIA
PHOTOLITHOGRAPHY FOTOMEC, TURIN
PRINTED IN THE MONTH OF NOVEMBER 2006
BY STAMPATRE, TURIN